Stories from Home
DOVER DAYS

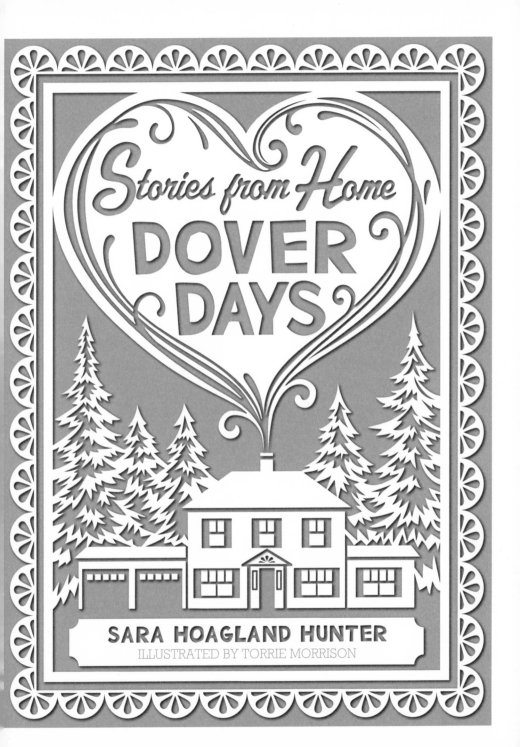

Stories from Home
DOVER DAYS

SARA HOAGLAND HUNTER

ILLUSTRATED BY TORRIE MORRISON

♥

FOR MUM, DAD, MANDY,
MOLLY, AND JOHN:
THE HOAGLANDS
OF HAVEN STREET

Pure humanity, friendship, home, the interchange of love,

bring to earth a foretaste of heaven.

Mary Baker Eddy

TABLE OF CONTENTS

17   ECHOES FROM THE FARMHOUSE

21   CRITTER CRISES

29   THE PLAYHOUSE

35   WHOSE RIGHT?

39   BUILDING THE STONE WALL

45   THE DANGER OF BOOKS

57   MY FIRST BEST FRIEND

63   THE WOODS

71   RAISING THE ROOFTOP

77   THE PINE TREE

83   SINGING DOWN THE MILES

93   THE TENNIS LADIES

PREFACE

Simple and true for we really lived most of it.

Louisa May Alcott—*Louisa May Alcott, Her Life, Letters, and Journals*
(ed. Ednah D. Cheney)

I guessed then, as the others did not, that this was our last real dinner together. After hundreds of school nights huddled around the antique, wooden table marked with mug rings and missing most of its original wooden pegs to secure the top, we had come to the end of the road. I was leaving for college in the morning. The remaining seats would empty over the next seven years—the raucous laughter and competition for Mom and Dad's attention fading until it was just the two of them reeling in wonderment at the two-decade whirlwind they had unleashed and survived.

I have always been a marker of moments—the need for dramatic closure running deep. Be it the final surveying of a classroom at the end of a school year with a montage of highlights playing in my head or my ritual New Year's Eve reading of the year's journal entries in front of the fire, I have ordered and appreciated life in chapters.

The chapter of family dinners around the old table was a long and formative one. Here, we had calibrated each day's crises with the measure of my father's gentle wisdom and humor. Here, my mother, so clear in her conviction of right versus wrong, had clickety clacked her high heels across the kitchen floor serving up dinner and life lessons night after night.

On that final night I halted my usual attempts to beat my siblings to a punchline and took a moment to freeze-frame the faces of five I would miss so much:

Mandy: a year and ten days my junior, my unconditional support and comic relief. Mom and Dad said we greeted each other with a look of delighted recognition the day she was born as if to say, "Finally!"

We know what the other is thinking with barely a raised eyebrow or flicker of a smile. As toddlers we had our own vocabulary. A few words imprinted themselves deeply enough to linger. "Ah-wee, ah-wee," was our satisfied refrain when pulling into the driveway after an absence from home. Perhaps we were echoing the comfort sounds of Mom and Dad saying, "Here we are." or "Now we are home." Whatever its origin, it represented a whole-souled sigh of rightness.

From a young age, my goal was to make Mandy laugh. One of my earliest memories is the sheer glee of discovering that if I climbed out my bedroom window and toddled across the roof, I could knock on Mandy's window and reduce her to a heap of giggles playing rooftop peek-a-boo. I still remember the icy calm instructions of my horrified parents when they discovered their four-year old scaling the roof in footsy pajamas. They coaxed me into the second-story window and summarily punished me but Mandy's laughs were always worth the penalty.

Molly: a born athlete whose physical and mental strength was early apparent. Molly could stand up to Mandy and me even as a toddler. She intimidated the heck out of John when he came along two years after her. Her steely, blue-eyed focus and sturdy frame made her a force—the sturdiness partly due to Mom's misreading of the baby formula instructions while preoccupied with Mandy and me (turns out she was imbibing the equivalent of straight whipped cream for months). Her formidable sense of order and unwavering moral conviction were as imposing as her strength. Although Mandy and I like to claim credit for molding her into the legendary head of school she is today (whipping lacrosse balls at her head, "borrowing" anything she valued), our methods of toughening her up were probably irrelevant. Her clarity and resolve were already apparent in her pre-school Christmas pageant when, as the angel of God, she bellowed, "Fear not!" to a pack of sniveling shepherds and a stunned audience.

Her drive and athletic prowess were balanced by deeply held principles of justice and honesty. This honed her skill at achieving exactly what she wanted while remaining within the letter of the law. One day at the beach, Mom was busy teaching Mandy and me how to swim and had enclosed John in his playpen. At a loss for what to do with Molly, she tied her to a stake planted above the tide line where she could play safely in the sand. Within minutes, Molly uprooted the stake, replanted it in the ocean and began swimming circles around it.

John, the long awaited baby boy, arrived when I was seven. He was the brother I read my favorite books to, the brother Molly dressed as a bride for Halloween, and the brother Mandy always beat to the joke. Actually, *he* always beat *her* to the joke but no one ever laughed until Mandy repeated it, causing him endless frustration.

A total tenderheart, he sobbed during *The Wizard of Oz* when Dorothy spied Auntie Em in the witch's crystal ball and couldn't get home. He bolted from the theatre when Butch and Sundance headed into a hail of bullets. On nighttime walks, he would warn us from his lookout spot atop Dad's shoulders to look straight ahead and not at the "Quarrel Bears."

Disciplining him proved a challenge to Mom and his teachers because, like Mandy, he could always make them laugh. Poor Dad had lined us up on the lawn one spring evening for a lecture on some infraction when John toddled behind him throwing new mown grass over his head like confetti. Dad's solemnity and futile, impassioned pleas to pay attention while grass fell from his head, nose, and mouth reduced us to helpless laughter.

When we three girls reached middle school and high school, Dad, ever the chivalrous romantic, would shake his head and say, "Women will never be a mystery to your brother."

This was usually in response to a shouting match about which sister had "pitted out" whose shirt or ruined the other's razor with her bristly legs. At least, we no longer shared a bathroom with the men.

One weekend when I was about eleven, we heard Dad downstairs hammering things and ripping out part of the kitchen wall. Sharing a bathroom with four women had finally taken its toll. I don't think he'd ever installed plumbing in his life but these were desperate times. He completed the downstairs bathroom in record time. The shower never produced more than a trickle and with no radiator, the toilet was like sitting on an iceberg in winter. No matter. Dad and John never set foot in the upstairs bathroom again.

The barrage of female dinner conversation was our lasting legacy to John. He has always been a best friend both to women and men, a brilliant observer of the nuances of human nature who can quote every favorite line from any book or movie of the last half-century. These days, he delivers a joke better than any of us. It is his punchlines we echo with admiration.

A few lines about my parents: Dad was a visionary and a prophet, a beautiful writer and clear thinker whose affection and belief in each one of us guaranteed the fulfilling of his expectation that our future was unlimited. Mom's spark and sparkle ignited in us a permanent love of life, friends, sports, nature, and, above all, home. Her conviction of God's presence freed us to lean on something surer than opinion or convention. Her insistence on daily joy and gratitude carries us through our days.

Someday I will preserve these precious growing up years in writing, I thought. And that is exactly what I have tried to do.

I would be remiss without sketching the sixth lead character of my childhood: the New England country town of Dover, Massachusetts. Infinitely greater than a backdrop, Dover was our dream-maker and friendship-provider in a world of fields and forests, brooks, streams, and the meandering Charles River, frozen and snow-covered in winter, muddy and melting in spring. We leapt from trees into crisp, crimson leaf piles in fall and flew across skating ponds stealing each other's hats in winter. We biked to the center of town under the guise of independence but always under the watchful eyes of neighbors who knew our phone number by heart. We attended the Chickering Elementary School where, as my Dad liked to joke, we "didn't even learn how to chicker." He maintained Dover was a "state of mind." I have to agree. To grow up rooted in love and sheltered by pines in a neighborhood where houses poured out kids for endless afternoons of fort building and game playing is to feel embraced for the many years to come.

CHAPTER ONE

ECHOES FROM THE FARMHOUSE

But Laura lay awake a little while, listening to Pa's fiddle softly

playing and to the lonely sound of the wind in the Big Woods...

She was glad that the cosy house, and Pa and Ma and the firelight

and the music, were now. They could not be forgotten, she

thought, because now is now. It can never be a long time ago.

Laura Ingalls Wilder — *Little House in the Big Woods*

Before there were words to pin down my memories, images floated through the farmhouse like the breeze through the thin, white curtains.

My father sings my sister and me to sleep in the lingering light of a summer's eve. It feels too early to be in bed when the new-mown field is lit by the setting sun. I must be just three and Mandy two because we are in the rented house with green shutters owned by the farmer at the top of the hill. Dad strums folk songs on the chocolate-colored guitar I still own—songs from a southern boyhood we don't understand but with melodies strangely comforting. His golden bass rings out tales of the "Birmingham jail", a train "a hundred coaches long", and a drunken sailor who must be put in the "long botillysober". I imagine the long botillysober to be the cavernous blanket chest at the end of my parents' bed that smells like mothballs and can crunch your fingers. Childhood is a state of wonder, trepidation, blind trust, and often complete puzzlement. With no frame of reference, what question could I possibly frame? Being closed in the dark, long botillysober seemed a dreadful punishment and made perfect sense. I actually regretted learning the real words a few years later. The lyrics: "Put him in the long boat 'til he's sober" may have dispersed the mists of childhood but they were far less exciting than imprisonment in the hollows of the finger-eating blanket chest.

There is much to be said for a life that begins with singing at bedtime. The cadences of my father's folk songs set the rhythm underlying all my days, instilling a love of poetry and a satisfaction in the resonance of phrases. It prepared the way for a love of the Beatitudes' simplicity and the perfection of an E.B. White sentence. It is why I still rush to my bedroom under the eaves to hear the rhythm of rain on rooftop, the coziest sound on earth.

"Watch the donut not the hole. Walk the lines and not the squares," he sang. What did it mean? I didn't question. Dad was singing at the foot of our bed about a sparrow who would take us to the rainbow. In the twilight glow of a room in a farmhouse, that was enough.

CHAPTER TWO

CRITTER CRISES

Life is always a rich and steady time when you are waiting for something to happen or to hatch.

E.B. White—*Charlotte's Web*

The dreamscape of the non-verbal years gave way to a gradual grapple with reality. Mysteries still abounded and the line between awake and asleep was often a fuzzy one. Many of my questions and nightmares revolved around large animals—all ours. A recurring nightmare featured our greyhound, Tanya, a looming mass of quivers and ribs. In the dream, she wore my father's tweed sports cap, smoked a pipe, and spoke in an ominous monotone, always with the same request: "Sara, come here and let me bite your hand."

I've never needed a psychiatrist to unravel the issue. The beast was four times my size and terrified me. Mom and Dad were pioneers in greyhound adoption and, with that inexplicable penchant of expectant parents to acquire dogs, had picked her up at the local racetrack before I was born. Tanya was no dignified champ retired after an illustrious string of victories but a veritable bundle of nerves who repeatedly jumped the starting gate or tripped over her own paws. Once, when Dad and I took her on a walk to Dover Center, she tripped and knocked her teeth out. As far as I knew, we were the only family to bring their dog to the town's orthodontist, a fact I found excruciatingly embarrassing.

Dad was disappointed when the braces proved to be no impediment to Tanya's habit of eating our neighbor's chickens. Her discovery of these tasty treats several years earlier had necessitated a phone call from Dad to our insurance agent that, as Mom recounted, went something like, "Jack Hoagland here. Say, does our policy cover damage to our car?…Good, good. How about the house?…Great and how about the neighbor's chickens our dog ate? Thank you so much."

Thus began a routine that played out for the next several years: Tanya eats neighbor's chickens. Neighbor reports in.

Dad files consumed chicken claim. Neighbor cashes check. Eat and repeat.

That dog was a victim of her own enthusiasm. She chased chickens, squirrels, children, and cars with equal abandon and poor results. One day, my mother ran her over. This wasn't noteworthy in itself; Mom had unwittingly nicked several of our pets. She bounded through life with the same enthusiasm as Tanya, juggling four kids, a dozen volunteer jobs, and her tennis matches. We always exited the drive-way in reverse, with pebbles and dust clouds flying. Tanya suffered only bruised toes (unlike Mandy's cat Tigger. RIP, Tigger). In Mom's defense, she always felt deep remorse and only hit a person once.

The Dover Police Chief, Bob Wilson, was a gentle man, at his happiest directing traffic through the town's only busy intersection between the drug store, gas station, and Town Hall. He greeted Dover's residents (all of whom he knew by name) by leaning back on his heels, raising his hand in a wave, and opening his mouth into a large silent "o". The day my mother backed out of the Town Hall parking lot onto his foot, his mouth formed the largest "O" I'd ever seen. When I pointed out she had hit the police chief, Mom jumped from the car apologizing profusely. He hurried her along. I think our family scared him.

His most frequent contact with us was through our donkey, Max, who was obsessed with the electric door at Higgins Foodland. Max regularly forded the fence surrounding our field, galloped through the woods to the center of town and parked himself on the rubber mat, opening the electric door to block foot traffic. He thrived on commotion and returned every few months for a fix.

In contrast, Chief Wilson dreaded any lapse in predictability and was thrown off balance by these donkey disturbances, forcing him to leave his post to calm the crowd at Higgins and move Max. Unlike Dover traffic, Max had no respect for order and interpreted every wave of the police chief's white glove as an invitation to dig in his hooves.

About once a month we would receive the inevitable phone call from the longsuffering chief, "Mrs. Hoagland, your donkey is blocking the electric door at Higgins again."

Mom would grab a neighbor or babysitter and a handful of carrots, pile us into the car, and ruminate aloud about why Max couldn't for once escape on a Saturday when Dad was home. By the time we pulled up, Max was in a giddy state—teeth bared and hee-hawing like crazy. On a good day, Mom could coax him off the mat before the editor of the Dover Suburban Press arrived with her camera to further humiliate us.

She would then ride him home while the neighbor delivered us. Mandy and I slid as far down into the backseat as possible while Molly greeted the crowd from her infant seat. John wasn't born yet and at those moments I wished I hadn't been either.

Another year, the fluffball chicks we received in our Easter baskets grew into psychotic roosters worthy of a Hitchcock movie. By then, Tanya had gone to the greyhound race track in the sky but I doubt even she would have dared eat them. My parents built a coop but, as usual, missed on essential proportions—this time, spatial. The nine growing, crowing roosters were assigned a plot under our pine tree appropriate for maybe one or two with no territorial instincts.

The resulting chicken wire death pit became the bane of my existence—teeming with screeching creatures who would attach to your body at a moment's notice and peck like maniacs just to amuse themselves.

We all cried when it was our turn to feed them. "They'll kill me and then you'll be sorry!" I protested.

"Don't be overdramatic," Mom would say, handing me ski goggles and a motorcycle helmet.

George, my brown and white hamster, was a gentler pet. I made the mistake of bringing him to the Thanksgiving table one year to show him off to the relatives. I begged Dad to pet him, forgetting about the juice on his fingers from carving the turkey. George lit into Dad with the full force of his needle-like hamster teeth and was instantly airborne. We couldn't find him anywhere.

A year later, Anna, our Norwegian au pair, complimented my mother on the clever American custom of storing small animals in the compost under the sink.

"Excuse me?" said Mom.

"You know. This one," said Anna opening the cabinet door to reveal George, inflated to ten times his original size. He blinked from the garbage pail with cheeks so fat his eyes looked like tiny, happy slits.

I don't miss the bizarre menagerie of my youth but I have gained a grudging admiration for my parents' collection of weird pets. Each day held the possibility of a call from the police chief, the risk of being blinded by a rabid rooster, or the discovery of a long-lost rodent under the sink. The house on Haven Street vibrated with critters and unpredictability. Nudged from my comfort zone to don a helmet to feed attack roosters or ride a rebellious donkey, each day required adaptability. Parents who gave me a donkey instead of a doll for my fourth birthday gave me an even bigger gift—a life of surprises.

CHAPTER THREE

THE PLAYHOUSE

I believe in imagination.

Meryl Streep

Our donkey Max was finally acquired by a 4-H Club boy who couldn't believe his good fortune in finding a free donkey that came with a year's supply of oats (Mom being eager to seal the deal.) Dad decided to turn the garage into something even less practical and more wonderful than a donkey stall...a theatre. Winter was fast approaching and the prospect of our neighborhood play rehearsals again moving into the house must have been powerful incentive to construct a stage elsewhere.

"Where will we park the car?" Mom asked, envisioning the endless season of snow, sleet, and sludge ahead.

"The driveway," said Dad. "Don't worry. I can always shovel it out."

There was no arguing with that. We witnessed his superhuman shoveling skills every time the Dover Fire Department blasted the "No School! Snow Day!" fire whistle. The same blast that caused us to bounce on our beds in ecstasy caused Dad to take flight. The concept of being trapped inside with all four of us plus the neighborhood gang powered his sputtering, gray Rambler through snowdrifts that would have intimidated Admiral Peary. Later when I studied Greek mythology and learned how Hercules' supernatural strength allowed him to clear thirty years of cow pies from a stable in record time, I thought of Dad.

Within a week, he had installed a wood floor over the concrete. Only the faintest odor of hay and gasoline remained. As always, Mom magnified the moment, suggesting we paint-spatter the new floor for a whimsical look. Arming us with paintbrushes and cans, she gave the glorious order to "Spatter!"

Say no more! We spattered the floor. We spattered each other. We spattered our rain ponchos beyond recognition.

The "victrola", as Mom insisted on calling it well into the digital age, was moved to the playhouse along with my parents' comprehensive collection of Broadway albums. We could all belt out songs from *The Music Man, Annie Get Your Gun, Guys and Dolls, Oklahoma, Carousel,* and *The Mikado* either when requested or, more often, when not.

When it came to mounting full-blown neighborhood productions, I was the self-appointed director.

The plays were adapted from whatever book I was reading at the time and usually included a musical number accompanied by a scratchy Broadway record album. I performed my one-man band at intermission with pots on my head, a recorder in my mouth, and a metal serving spoon in hand.

The inevitable playdate guests were cast as Grandma and Grandpa Nellypoops—non-speaking roles which made use of the vinyl wigs Mom had ordered from Sears for our dress-up trunk.

My casting decisions went unquestioned until the day my classmate, chief competitor and closest neighborhood friend, Betsy Piper, cracked. In *The Three Bears Meet Grandma and Grandpa Nellypoops,* I announced that Molly with her long braids would play Goldilocks, Betsy and her siblings would be bears, and Mandy's playdate, Prudy, and one of the neighborhood boys would stumble through as Grandma and Grandpa Nellypoops.

Betsy, a towhead blonde four years Molly's senior, accurately accused me of sibling favoritism and stomped from the playhouse yelling, "You are not the boss!"

The younger kids blinked. Betsy's little brother, Jamie, began to cry. I quieted the rumbling, "She'll be back." (a sure bet since Mrs. Piper kept the door locked until dinner time.)

When Betsy returned, I feigned largesse and gave her the lead. Truth is, in the ten minutes she'd been gone, I'd realized Molly's skipping and whistling-through-the-forest skills weren't up to my standards.

An hour later, we rounded up our usual audience of mothers, pets, and Mrs. Viannay, an ancient woman from down the street with a dog-whistle pitched voice and thick European accent. We couldn't understand her but she always seemed pleased to be included.

The action was flawed from the start. Prudy shuffled across the stage on cue as Grandma Nellypoops but lost control the moment Grandpa Nellypoops teetered towards her in search of an embrace. The more severely I glared from the wings, the deeper the abyss of uncontrollable laughter into which she plummeted. Much to Betsy's and my irritation, the production was a shambles long before Goldilocks could utter a word. The daily drama that played out on that stage as our neighborhood cast of characters elbowed for position is upstaged in my memory by the laughter—the blessed, body-racking, gasping-for-air laughter.

CHAPTER FOUR

WHOSE RIGHT?

You never really understand a person until you consider

things from his point of view.

Harper Lee—*To Kill A Mockingbird*

Whenever I am flummoxed by the inability of others to see my justifiably entrenched point of view, I think back to a lesson learned in the bathtub at age six. Mandy and I had just been taught our right from our left in kindergarten and first grade at Dover's Chickering School. Eager to flaunt our newfound knowledge, we held up our right hands to practice. The problem was we were facing each other in the tub.

"This is the right," I proclaimed with big sister assurance.

"No," said Mandy undeterred and raising the opposite hand. "This is."

I reached for the part in my hair on the right side of my head. "You're wrong, dummy," I said splashing her. "That's left."

"No, *you're* wrong, stupid head," she said poking my right hand. "That's left."

A full-blown, hair yanking, arm pinching, water fight erupted until Mom came running.

"What on earth is going on?" she cried, sloshing across the floor to tear us apart.

Through tears of certainty and frustration, we each detailed the other's ignorance.

"Tell her who's right, Mom!" I begged.

Wait...what was this? Mom was laughing! Worse, she then uttered a most dissatisfying answer. "You both are."

Mandy and I were suspect. Mom tried to explain the importance of point of view but we weren't ready to hear it. How could something as definite as right and left depend on one's position in a bathtub? I was annoyed she wouldn't declare me totally right and Mandy totally wrong. A tie during bitter competition is utterly deflating.

That tub scene plays out frequently in my head these days. Temperatures rise on the global scene as views bifurcate, then ossify—each opinion stiff with self-justification. I think about Mom who simply loved and delighted in each of us, regardless of our limited perspectives. Her unchanging maternal love and exalted view provided a glimpse into the nature of the one divine Parent who sees and loves us all.

CHAPTER FIVE

BUILDING THE STONE WALL

She held the whole world of flowers in a warm embrace.

E.B. White—Introduction to *Onward and Upward in the Garden*
by Katharine White

For my mother, money was something to be stretched not feared. The "cookies" she served us after school were actually saltines—a fact I learned the hard way when I thanked a friend's mother for the delicious cookies and her whole family burst out laughing.

Mom sewed and re-sewed our clothing as it moved down the line from sister to sister. I was lucky to be the oldest but even my clothes were often hand-me-downs from family friends. In the five years required for the jeans, sweaters, and dresses to reach Molly, they were reimagined and repatched to the point where they ignited her lifelong passion to buy, own, and preserve her own things with meticulous care. To this day, her taste in new shoes and her work ethic are both impeccable—honed by years of babysitting and yard work to afford clothes untouched by sisters' hands.

Mom's resourcefulness impacted all of us. One Christmas, we awoke to find six pairs of wooden skis under the tree. She'd bought them tired and scratched at the Dover Country Store, our local junk and penny candy shop, then sanded and repainted them a jaunty blue. Our family's love of skiing was instant and has enriched the experience of three generations thanks to Mom's initial seventy-two dollar investment.

One morning, she herded us into the family station wagon for yet another adventure. Tires squealed. Gravel flew. She confided in us four kids as co-conspirators. Rocks had been cleared from a site on the nearby banks of the Charles River to make way for the construction of a mansion. Instead of joining the mournful chorus of suburban whiners bemoaning the invasion of Dover by the nouveau riche, she embraced opportunity. "I can finally build a stone wall by the garden! Won't it be spectacular with purple, white, and fuchsia phlox?"

We nodded, not because we knew what phlox was but because her enthusiasm elicited yesses from all who knew her. She stepped harder on the gas with each detail, singing. "We'll have pansies! We'll have hollyhocks! We'll have petunias!"

We nodded and gripped the armrests.

At the construction site, she charmed the steam shovel operator right out of his vehicle. Just like us, he was under her spell as she described her vision for the new garden wall. Soon, he too was searching for the right boulders to "drip with phlox". We trudged and dragged and pushed and lifted until the rear bumper hovered inches above the ground. On the way home, the undercarriage scraped the pavement each time we encountered a bump.

By the time we met Dad at the commuter train, we were a sticky, tired mess. My enthusiasm for Mom's dream garden was on the wane until, in preparation for the mountainous task awaiting him at home, she asked Dad, "You know that plant we talked about getting each other for our anniversary?"

"The bleeding heart?" he answered.

This sounded promising. "What's a bleeding heart?" I asked.

"It's an exquisite shade plant with tiny pink hearts hanging from each stem," she said. "I've always loved them. They look absolutely stunning set off by a New England stone wall."

Dad slowed down and smiled at her in the passenger seat. "Do I have a choice?"

"Nope!" we all shouted at the top of our lungs.

My parents built the stone wall together, patiently selecting and fitting each stone in place. They tilled the ground and edged the beds in time for their June anniversary. The bleeding heart was the first to be planted.

I was secretly disappointed. A plant with a great name like "bleeding heart" should have dripped red and been as menacing as a Venus Flytrap. But Mandy marveled at the perfectly shaped hearts and couldn't resist fingering them.

As we grew, Mom's vision took shape. Lush pink and deep

purple phlox covered the stones and the garden beds burst with lilies, bluebells, violets, and black-eyed Susans. The bleeding heart remained Mom's favorite… "a focal point," she called it.

Decades later, Molly and I surprised Mandy with a return visit to our childhood home for her birthday. The owner was as pleased to show us what had changed as we were to see what hadn't. A shockingly blue pool dominated the field where Max had roamed and we'd played kickball, Red Rover, Spud, and Sardines. The pine tree we'd climbed each afternoon was stripped of all but a few dead branches but the stone wall stood as solid as the spring my parents built it.

Mom's flowers were gone but I thought about the gardens each of my siblings has nurtured. Like Mom, Molly has been known to garden under the stars—her great release after a demanding work day. John tends wildflowers and an orchard in view of his home office and raises summer vegetables as Mom did in the backyard. Mandy has planted a bleeding heart at every house she's ever lived in—a focal point of continued good.

CHAPTER SIX

THE DANGER
OF BOOKS

And best of all, the wilderness of books, in which she could

wander where she liked, made the library a region of bliss to her.

Louisa May Alcott—*Little Women*

I was swept away by the entire experience of reading a book by myself for the first time—from the march down the school corridor into the sun-filled library to the actual reading of the book which still seems the most radical act of independence available on the planet.

The responsibility of choosing just one from among the gleaming parade of books jacketed in official library plastic was daunting. After a heart-pounding perusal of the low, second-grade tables, I reached for *Little Tim and the Brave*

Sea Captain by Edward Ardizzone. The cover illustration of the gray-green tidal wave sloshing over a listing ocean liner looked to be a serious and dramatic choice. Gripping it as my most precious possession, I moved at a gait just shy of the forbidden "running" to the line at the check-out desk. Finally, with a satisfying pound of the librarian's date stamp, the book was mine. I thrust it deep into my green book bag and bounced up and down waiting for the dismissal bell and the buses mercifully lined up to carry us home.

Alone on my bed, I entered a whole new world that included just Little Tim and me. Propelled into the catastrophe and melancholy of the ship's capsizing, I felt as giddily solitary as Tim himself. In some ways, I've been adrift ever since; for while books have been my salvation, they have perpetually landed me in a boatload of trouble.

When I was eight, I ran away from home à la Tom Sawyer. I tied a handkerchief full of supplies (saltines, peanut butter, knife) to a dead pine branch , filled my Roy Rogers thermos with leftover breakfast coffee and set out across our field towards the forest, stopping to fortify myself with a swig from the thermos as I imagined Tom had done. Yuck! This first taste of discrepancy between romance and reality was particularly bitter. How could Tom stand this stuff? In order to measure up to my mentor, I gamely swigged and hiked and hiked and swigged until I felt so grim I had to swallow my pride before I lost my lunch. Heading for home and staggering in the door, I couldn't even wallow in the welcome I'd imagined for a long-lost runaway. No one noticed I'd been gone for twenty minutes. What Mom did notice was that I had wrecked one of Dad's good handkerchiefs with pine sap and peanut butter. Worse than the embarrassment or the stomach ache was a malaise I wouldn't be able to describe until many years and disappointments later – the cloying fear that real life might not measure up to book life.

This acrid taste of reality was subsumed by our family's weekly trip to the Dover Town Library. As soon as I pulled open the heavy green doors, I entered that hushed world of imagination and possibility that set me aflutter. In the cool semi-darkness, glamorous high school students hovered over homework at a long mahogany table lit by brass lamps with green shades. Peering from her formidable desk, Mrs. Bertschi, the white haired librarian, shushed and stamped. I inhaled the scent of shelves packed floor to ceiling with books that enveloped me in new worlds of adventure. In the ensuing years, I consumed every picture book in the children's corner and went on to devour the orange biography series on the chapter book wall. I didn't just *read* about my heroes, Molly Pitcher, Abe Lincoln, and Madame Curie; I became them.

Thomas Alva Edison had a particular effect. After reading his biography, I begged for, and miraculously received, a Gilbert Chemistry set for Christmas. The two-sided wooden case displayed rows of enticing bottles alphabetized from aluminium ammonium sulfate to zinc sulfate. There were test tubes, beakers, flasks, and tubing. Happily relegated to the basement, I became a mad scientist. In those carefree days before lawyers discovered the potential of the toy market, the introductory experiments taught me how to turn water into wine with sodium carbonate and how to set a dollar bill on fire with rubbing alcohol. When Mom smelled the flames and came running, she told me our family needed "no help burning through money, thank you."

Once I exhausted the experiments in the instruction manual, I emulated my hero, Thomas Alva, swapping all the bottle labels for skull and crossbones labels I drew myself. My lab work centered on creating stink bombs to impress the neighborhood boys. With no labels to guide me, these morphed into foaming, lava-like substances that often scared even me. I was secretly relieved when the bottles ran out and my parents refused to order the refresher kit.

Perhaps no less risky was my obsession with my fictional heroes. Lucinda, the heroine of Ruth Sawyer's *Roller Skates,* sent me careening down the pot-holed streets of Dover. How I longed to glide over her Manhattan sidewalks in old-fashioned, high-top roller skates impressing vendors and befriending all in my path. Instead, I was reduced to hopping over our gravel driveway, launched out of metal skates with useless clamps that refused to grip my sneakers. The skates turned into angry, flailing bear traps bound to my shins, each time I attempted a graceful glide. Why couldn't they behave like Lucinda's alluring lace-up boots in the illustration?

For a while, the gap I experienced between fiction and reality only resulted in skinned knees, tummy aches, and a bruised ego but as the books became more captivating, my escapades ventured into riskier territory. My tomboy heroines from Caddie Woodlawn to Jo March inspired the toughening up of my younger sisters—all for their own good of course— with my "Tomboy Tests". These ranged from launches off the swingset at peak arc to scaling the garage roof. The tests shared the common ingredient of jumping off of things...the higher the better. The capstone was to jump from the play-house roof onto our snow-covered terrace with extra points for landing on one's knees—my serious miscalculation being the depth of the snow and Molly's dedication. She still bears the scar and reminds me of my insistence that she didn't need to tell Mom.

There was one shining moment when life finally lived up to art. In search of a shortcut to the skating pond, my siblings and I were battling our way through knee-deep snow and whiplashing branches in the thickest part of our woods. We rarely veered from the established paths because the low tangle of pine boughs snapping in our eyes made it impossible. But that day we were a determined army. Skates slung over our shoulders, we plowed a path with our boots, each whomping the one behind us with a snow-covered branch. We were about to give up when the sky lightened and my favorite book came to life.

I idolized the mishaps, adventures, holidays, and traditions of the five siblings in *Whirligig House* by Anna Rose Wright. At that moment, Chapter One, "Devil's Chute", about a sledding hill flanked by a narrow chute, rose before our eyes.

"Devil's Chute!" I shouted, heading for the slope of the kamikaze flume. The other kids quickly opted for the more inviting slope of the wide sledding hill but I grabbed Mandy and pulled her toward the narrower path.

"You are cute Cricket, the middle sister in *Whirligig House*," I instructed. "I'm your oldest sister Nan and when you become wedged in the gully, I will rescue you."

Suspicious but agreeable, Mandy perched in her slippery snow pants staring at the sheer drop. I gave her a shove from a running start. The problem was she was too skinny to wedge, and plummeted like a human luge, accelerating until an overhanging branch snatched the hood of her coat in a death grip. In a daring rescue, I slid down the chute and unzipped the coat before she turned purple. We shot to the bottom where she lay gasping and shivering in the snow before we decided to do it again.

The sledding hill became a valued neighborhood destination teeming with toboggans and flying saucers after a snowstorm. Devil's Chute was reserved for only the bravest and skinniest among us. When we discovered our piano teacher lived on the other side of the hill, Mandy and I made a practice of sliding down on our piano books as a shortcut home. This made for a great ride when the chute was icy but did a number on our piano books and tailbones.

The books that landed me in worse trouble were the Nancy Drew mysteries. The Stratmeyer Syndicate, parading under the pen name of Carolyn Keene, was a mob who really knew how to write. They lured me with enticing titles like *The Password to Larkspur Lane, The Clue of the Velvet Mask*, and *The Mystery at the Moss-Covered Mansion.*

My downfall was *The Bungalow Mystery.*

After reading it, I discovered a bungalow in our woods. How had I missed it?

"This bungalow is a hideout for criminals," I announced to my assistants Mandy, Molly, Betsy, and her younger sister Gwen.

"What's a bungalow?" asked Mandy.

"A secret cabin hiding stolen goods or a kidnap victim," I patiently explained.

"It's Jack Monroe's tool shed," said Betsy, unimpressed.

"Do those look like tools?" I whispered pointing to the white bags stashed in the corner.

In the autumn twilight, peering into a shadowy bungalow deep in the forest, I was Nancy Drew, super sleuth of River

Heights. "The burglars will be coming back for those. We need to remove them."

A hush fell over the group as I picked up a brick. "Well, what are you waiting for?" I asked.

Evidently, for me to throw the first brick. After the first shock of shattering glass, the others joined in and smashed with gusto. We obtained multiple entry points but as the trials of a super sleuth would have it, just as we were about to sneak in, the dreaded dinner bell rang.

The Pipers ran home. Mandy and I meandered—the clang of the bell having awakened a queasy sensation of incoming guilt. Molly ran her little legs off toward dinner and I should have known then the weasel was about to give us up.

Snuggled next to Mom in the kitchen alcove by the time we arrived, she trembled with excitement. As Dad sat down, she announced, "Sara told us to break Jack Monroe's windows."

The hidden bungalow faded in the glare of Mom and Dad's inquiry.

"Is this true?" asked Dad.

No sense risking another book ban for my "over-active imagination." I nodded and took the consequences.

In time, I recovered from the humiliation of the in-person apology to Jack Monroe and the six weeks of chores to pay for the window replacements. I even made peace with Molly. But I'm not sure I ever made peace with the gap between a beautiful word like bungalow and a boring, old tool shed.

CHAPTER SEVEN

MY FIRST
BEST FRIEND

Wilbur never forgot Charlotte…none of the new spiders ever

quite took her place in his heart. She was in a class by herself.

It is not often that someone comes along who is a true friend

and a good writer. Charlotte was both.

E.B. White— *Charlotte's Web*

Ihere is nothing quite so magical as the wonder of a first best friend. Outside the familiar context and confines of those assigned you through geographic or genetic proximity is the friend you discover for yourself…the one who saves you a seat on the bus, makes you laugh until you can't breathe, and the one you look for at recess. Mine was Margery Adams.

We met the spring before kindergarten on the slope of the Dover Town Hall lawn at the annual end-of-school rite, the Chickering School Folk Festival. I envied Margery who waved to her older siblings marching and dancing in the show. As the oldest, I had no siblings to watch. Mom must have brought me as an introduction to the school I would be starting in the fall or maybe as a treat after being stuck indoors with chicken pox for two weeks. Our mothers knew each other because everyone knew each other in Dover. They chatted and told us we would be in the same class in the fall. Margery had a nice smile and admired my twirly skirt with the sparkles Mom and Dad had bought me in Mexico. School was suddenly looking a lot more promising.

For the next six years, we were inseparable. I spent countless afternoons riding the school bus to Margery's house in a wooded corner of town dotted with the farms and summer retreats of old, distinguished Boston families. Her father's name on the mailbox, J.Q. Adams, held historical significance for my parents but I just knew him as Margery's kind dad. We invented ritual games for the trek up her private country lane. One involved a ledge shelf we dubbed "The Judge's Rock" where we took turns hearing cases from each other about someone we didn't like at school or an invented criminal activity. From the imposing vantage point atop the rock, whoever of us was serving as judge for the day listened solemnly to the complaint and doled out the verdict and appropriate punishment. Years later, Margery used her degree from Harvard Law School to fight to protect the beauty of our home territory as an environmental lawyer. I often thought back to the Judge's Rock and the early decisions rendered by an earnest elementary-schooler.

The Adams' mudroom was lined with webbed-footed boots with lace-up tops. Wish I'd know then to invest in the weird looking boots that launched the L.L. Bean mail order empire. More impressive were the wooden cases filled with bottles of ginger ale and Coca Cola. Coming from a home stocked only with orange juice and milk, I was awestruck. After-school snacks here were a revelation. Mrs. Adams, a sweet tooth herself, introduced me to the greatest food group ever when she scooped a dollop of vanilla ice cream into my ginger ale. My first ice cream soda!

Propelled by snacks, we burst out the back door and played outside until dark. We swung on the tire swing in the towering oak and jumped into piles of blazing orange and red maple leaves in fall. We tobogganed on the hill that bordered the nearest neighbor in winter. In spring, we walked to Granny Adams' farm to see the lambs cared for by Mr. Cronin, a pink-cheeked Irishman with a melodious voice and a smile for everyone in Dover. On the rare days when it was too cold to play outside, we made popcorn, played endless board games, and lost ourselves in the latest Nancy Drew mystery.

It was at Margery's I spent my first night away from home and at Margery's I learned there was no Santa Claus. She was a tenderheart and broke it to me gently. When I mentioned some dummy in our class who didn't believe in Santa, she said, "I believe there is a spirit of Santa Claus." It was clear she took no glee in imparting this less than satisfying news. I have always appreciated that.

A highlight list of events cannot capture the nature of a friendship forged from the spontaneity and sheer pleasure of unplanned childhood afternoons. One photo remaining from that era comes close. Mom must have recognized the preciousness of two ten-year olds at a moment in time and snapped the picture. Margery and I lie in our meadow smiling beneath a glorious canopy of apple blossoms blooming in the orchard behind us. It must have been May during that one excruciatingly brief week when New England's fruit trees are in full flower—as fragrant and fleeting as the joys of childhood and as miraculous as a first best friend.

CHAPTER EIGHT

THE WOODS

So they went off together. But wherever they go, and whatever happens to them on the way, in that enchanted place on the top of the Forest, a little boy and His Bear will always be playing.

A.A. Milne—*The House At Pooh Corner*

A wall of towering pines marked the line of demarcation between the field of sunshine where we played endless games with the neighborhood gang and a shadier world of forts, forest, and secret paths once trod by Indian moccasins. Every boulder hid the possibility of spotted salamanders ("mud puppies" we called them) to be captured for our terrariums. Every hole we shoveled held the possibility of buried treasure. Our collections included fragments of blue and white colonial crockery, a pewter fork, arrowheads, and tattered canvas from an ancient tent.

The winding paths led to different destinations—all of them exciting. There was the path to the sledding hill, the path to the town skating pond, and, best of all, the path that beckoned us each Friday to our dream destination on the other side of the woods: the penny candy store. The Dover Country Store had served as a quaint and cozy train station until the car-buying boom of the 1950s and '60s when the lure of a private commute from our rural outpost ran the rails out of business.

An energetic entrepreneur had since turned the depot into a repository for the used junk of everyone in town and dubbed it an antique store. Here, you could find warped tennis rackets, bed springs, typewriters, an old sleigh or a rusted weather vane if you dared brave the sky-high piles of the station's former waiting room. The wooden shelves groaned with trinkets: china dogs, door stops, glass bottles, pins from presidential campaigns, and ancient postcards. None of these items impressed us except as a musty, dusty background to the paradise of shimmering candy cases lining the wall by the cash register. Mrs. Dowd filled each of our small, brown paper bags with our earnestly selected favorites. Mine were mint juleps, candy buttons, fireballs, red licorice, jaw breakers, spearmint leaves and Pixie Sticks. I scorned Mandy's purchase of hideous, orange marshmallow circus peanuts, Whoppers, Milk Duds, and canker-producing candy necklaces. Once our bags were filled, we would dash back to our most recently constructed fort and munch, trade, and giggle to our heart's content. The joke of puffing on bubble gum cigarettes or sporting red wax candy lips never disappointed. Neither did the contests to see who could suck on a fireball the longest, whose jawbreaker turned the most colors, or whose tongue could turn the most sickeningly red, green or purple.

Some of our forts and hideouts were, in retrospect, just plain dangerous. The trees bore scars of our attempted treehouses.

Wood scraps pilfered from kindling piles were nailed into trunks to serve as steps. These were only loosely nailed and led to branches that couldn't hold the weight of a wren.

The riskiest fort we ever built wasn't in the trees; it was below ground. Inspired by a rotting, wooden door, still in its frame, we found deep in the woods, we shoveled a four foot pit and widened its sides until Mandy, Betsy, and I could crouch in the depths of a highly unstable situation. We then laid the door snugly over the top, creating the perfect trap door entrance to our secret club. Descending with flashlights and shutting the door overhead, we couldn't believe our brilliance. No one would ever discover us, least of all Wendell, Tory, or any of the numerous, cootie-contaminated neighborhood boys we loved to hate.

In the glorious weeks before our little brothers wrecked it, we shared secrets, Tomboy Club meetings, and each other's penny candy. Our younger brothers, John and Jamie, were always wrecking our forts. This might have been because they were too small to build one themselves, too annoying ever to be allowed entrance, too non-verbal to argue their case for inclusion, or more likely, because boys just have fun wrecking things. When we discovered the door submerged in a massive cave-in, I comforted myself with the thought of a future generation of neighborhood kids rediscovering the door and resuming the inevitable cycle of building and wrecking.

Our masterpiece was the teepee Mandy, Molly, John, and I built one April Saturday when a hint of spring was in the air and our parents had abandoned us with a babysitter we were desperate to escape. Taking to the woods, we gathered the longest pine boughs we could find and bound them at the top with Mom's clothesline rope. After fanning out the boughs to form the scaffolding, we gathered armfuls of twigs to cover the frame. Molly and John filled a wheelbarrow with the pine needles that carpeted the forest floor and chucked them at the frame while Mandy and I reached to pat them in place. An ancient section of picket fence served as our front gate.

I cherish the photo Dad took of the four of us clustered inside our teepee, grinning with pride. We are the picture of childhood Saturdays in Dover: carefree, cared for, overjoyed.

When I first read the poetry of Robert Frost, I thought he must have explored our woods. They were "lovely, dark, and deep" with just the right blend of light and dark, promise and mystery. Except for the disappointment of not being able to ride the birches as successfully as the protagonist of his poem, *Birches*, neither our woods nor Frost's poems ever let me down. Trudging home from skating or sledding on late winter afternoons, I often stopped in a grove of pines, surrounded by snow-laden branches in my own, private sanctuary. Twilight's quiet descent added to the atmosphere of sacred solitude. I never failed to repeat *Stopping by Woods on a Snowy Evening* until the last rays poked through the trees and the melancholy echo of "miles to go before I sleep" nudged me home. At the edge of the meadow, the distant silhouettes of my parents moving through the light of the kitchen window drew me toward dinner and the warmth of a family awaiting my arrival—a view I expect and hope to see again some day.

CHAPTER NINE

RAISING THE ROOFTOP

I am in the garret with my papers round me, and a pile of

apples to eat while I write my journal, plan stories, and enjoy the

patter of rain on the roof, in peace and quiet.

Louisa May Alcott—Journal entry April, 1885

I always loved acting out plays and inventing stories. In second grade, I began to write them down. When, after reading a few, my grandmother singled me out to accompany her to Orchard House, the home of writer Louisa May Alcott, I was enchanted. My cousins, siblings, and I had previously experienced our artist grandmother more as an energy field leaving jolted households in her wake than as a grandmother you actually did things with. She squeezed art classes, book writing, piano playing, craft-making, and summer camp administration into days that were never long enough.

I huddled in the back seat as she careened over the country roads between Dover and Concord, Massachusetts. One hand on the wheel, she held up the pine cones and greens piled on the front seat, showing me how they would be Christmas wreaths in no time.

The Alcotts' quaint family kitchen at Orchard House was bathed in a heavenly light, possibly due to my relief at having arrived alive. The wooden kitchen table where the four sisters of *Little Women* gathered for Christmas dinner was exactly as I had pictured, right down to the basket of apples. I was drawn to the parlor with Beth's piano and the curtain ready to pull for family plays but it was upstairs in Louisa's bedroom, where my destiny was decided. Winter light fell across the smudged pages of a well-worked manuscript at a simple, wooden writing desk by the window. I couldn't imagine a more perfect future.

From that day forward, I cherished my dream and copied a diary entry of Louisa's into my own: "I am in the garret with my papers round me, and a pile of apples to eat while I write my journal, plan stories, and enjoy the patter of rain on the roof, in peace and quiet."

Two years later, in an alignment of hope, expectation, and reality, my father made a stunning announcement. We were raising the rooftop! Mandy and I would be moved to the attic so our brother John could have his own bedroom. I was ecstatic! Never mind the intense odor of mothballs or that you had to duck under head-banging eaves. I readied my journals and notebooks for my studio in the sky. Dad had hired a carpenter to install dormer windows overlooking field and forest. I could hardly wait.

The carpenter was a wizened, figure with glittering brown eyes and a charming smile—a benign Rumpelstiltskin named Mr. Jordan. His overall pockets bulged with boxes of Good 'n Plenty. We delighted in his liberal distribution of candy and tall tales (the tallest of which, Dad said, was the time estimated to complete the job). We crowded around his stepladder chewing our treats as he spoke from on high. He was our hero and he had hit on a sure-fire method of job protection. The more impatient Dad became, the more candy and stories Mr. Jordan shared.

When the day finally arrived for the raising of the roof, we assembled on the lawn and squinted into the spring sun as he lifted and propped the roof with space to install the windows. I'd be able to see over the treetops!

Mandy and I moved into our sky palace a few weeks later and whispered long into the night from our beds snuggled in opposite corners.

"For the umpteenth time, quiet down, girls," Mom called. But this was the beginning of years of nighttime rituals not even Mom could halt. We played flashlight tag on the ceiling. We invented the "Initial Game", stumping each other with the initials of celebrities and school friends. In December, we curled up in blankets by the open windows to hear the Christmas carols wafting across the woods from the Dover Church bell tower. Sometimes, I wrote late into the night at my desk by the window. We ended each night with our sister sign-off, affectionately abbreviated "All Four Things" (Good night. I love you. Pray for each other. See you in the morning.)

If one of us couldn't sleep, we would wake the other. On one of these nights, we discovered a mystery we have never been able to solve.

Padding to the window in my pjs, I detected the twinkle of a light deep in the forest. "Mandy, come here and look at this!"

Mandy dutifully joined me at the window. Where was that light coming from? There weren't any houses or streets in that direction—just a sea of treetops. For nights afterward, we would run to the window to check on our light. It was always there, twinkling through the trees even when I set my alarm for two a.m. No matter how early we rose in the morning, it was extinguished. After numerous Saturday morning missions through the woods to locate its source, we finally gave up and gave in to its wonder and mystery. We dubbed it "The Welcoming Light", our promise of comfort—the light shining in darkness as sure as our forever friendship forged under the eaves.

CHAPTER TEN

THE PINE TREE

They all said 'Hallo,'' and felt awkward and unhappy suddenly,

because it was a sort of good-bye they were saying, and they

didn't want to think about it.

A.A. Milne—*The House at Pooh Corner*

In the early 1960s, every neighborhood was made up of houses exploding with children whose ages were interlaced with our own and who, like us, were locked out of the house until the dinner bell rang. Besides our games and plays and fort building, the pine tree in our backyard was a premium neighborhood attraction. It towered several stories above our house with a perfect array of branches for even the least adventurous climber. Its limbs were as tiered as our elementary school reading groups. My parents had built a sandbox around the base of the thick, sap-stained trunk for my brother John and his pre-school friends. There must have been 500 match-box cars in there. I embedded them in my feet every time I jumped barefoot to the sand. John and his friends engaged in endless road or canal construction, depending on the season and the availability of Mom's garden hose.

Above the heads of the preschoolers dangled the legs of the six and seven-year-olds who swung, chatted, and bounced in the long, low, bending branches led by my sis-ter Molly, braids flying, who could always bounce the high-est. Sometimes they pretended to ride great, galloping horses but for anyone beyond second grade this was sissy stuff. We sixth-graders yanked our way to the top branches as fast as monkeys until we ran out of perches. I envied Betsy's dexterity and wiry compactness especially now that I'd grown as gan-gly as Popeye's Olive Oyl. My stork legs insured I beat her in running races but made it impossible to follow her into the best hiding places or the crook of a treetop. Mandy had it even worse. Not only were her legs endlessly long and skinny, she had to prove to Betsy and me that being a year younger she could still keep up. One day, she overdid it and attempted a foothold on a twig. There was a crack, then a yell as we watched her bounce backwards through the thick boughs which only slightly broke her fall. When she landed in the sandbox, she made a noise that sounded like, "Thwug."

Mom, who had witnessed the calamity from the kitchen window came running.

Mandy gasped for air like a beached flounder.

"She's dead," said Molly.

"Nonsense," said my mother, always calm in the face of disaster. "She's just had the wind knocked out of her."

Mandy's writhing made it apparent to all of us that having the wind knocked out of you was a fate worse than death. Even our male classmates who had come to the yard to start a pine cone war were uncharacteristically somber and impressed.

When Mandy finally managed great gulps of air, Mom hugged her and went back inside to finish getting dinner ready. With the closing of the kitchen door, childhood rules were again in play. Mandy yanked Molly out of the tree for having proclaimed her premature death. The matchbox boys pig-piled on top of them—ever resentful of the low-bough-dwellers just out of reach. The older boys used the melee as their cue to pepper us with their pine cone arsenal.

Betsy and I chased them to halt the firestorm. I had a crush on one half my size with green eyes and a smattering of freckles. He was the smartest, most athletic person in our grade—a title I'd competed for since kindergarten. My fifth-grade growth spurt meant I could pin him to the ground, which I did that day, smugly assuming I'd earn his respect. Although our academic rivalry continued until the end of high school, our physical competition died then and there, leaving me as deflated as Mandy when she hit the ground. He ceased wriggling long enough to utter the words that effectively ended childhood and welcomed me to the murk of adolescence. "You're never gonna get the boys to like you this way."

I pretended not to care but was horrified to realize I did! I had entered a world where status was no longer measured by how high I could climb a tree or how many boys I could beat up. The clear calculations of simple math had sadly been usurped by the mysteries of chemistry.

CHAPTER ELEVEN

SINGING DOWN THE MILES

It was a grass harp, gathering, telling, a harp of voices

remembering a story.

Truman Capote—*The Grass Harp*

What year did we stop singing in the car…not with the radio or digital backup but with the voices of family and friends on the way to New Hampshire ski slopes or Cape Cod summers or our annual trek to Florida?

I remember when we started. I was four when Mom asked Mandy and me if we wanted to see Mighty Mouse dance. Really?! Mighty Mouse was a light beige Pontiac with round fenders and large, friendly headlights. Named after our favorite cartoon character, the car lived in the second stall of the garage next to our pet donkey Max.

On that particular day, I wish I could write that we were tucked into car seats; but we were most likely roaming the car playing with the manual door lock buttons and metal ash trays, or sticking our heads out the window. This was a seatbeltless era and even if it hadn't been, the mothers were exponentially outnumbered by their baby boom babies and felt they had achieved enough just wrestling that many toddlers into a car.

No sooner had we shouted our desire for the car to dance than Mighty Mouse plunged forward, then halted, then plunged forward again to the rhythm of Mom's jaunty singing. The jerks and spasms weren't exactly like any dancing we'd experienced but it was spectacular!

"More!" we pleaded when he came finally came to a stop.

"I guess we're not singing loud enough,"said Mom.

Say no more. We bellowed with reckless abandon as Mighty Mouse's rhumba resumed. We bounced ourselves breathless, never noticing that Mom was controlling the dance. That was her gift…to transform life's mundane moments into flights of joy without us ever seeing her work the pedals.

My parents were a match made in music. Dad sang his way through Yale, first as President of the Freshman Glee Club and later as a member of the select senior dozen, the Whiffenpoofs, whose voices and lives would blend in harmony for the next five decades. He met Mom on a Yale-Smith singing weekend with her Smith College a cappella group, escaping his pre-arranged date as soon as he spotted the sparkling, brown-eyed beauty bursting with spirit and vitality. Mom was equally smitten with the tall, lean, sandy-haired bass whose gentle manner reflected his southern upbringing and whose twinkle and sense of humor sparkled in her presence. She always said the first thing she noticed about him were the laugh crinkles around his eyes. Sally Ray and Jack Hoagland were soon an item, burning up the road between Northampton and New Haven on weekends and causing Dad to throw caution and academics to the wind.

In later years, at Yale reunions, we were alternately proud and mortified when the "Whiffs" were trotted out and Dad was requested to reprise his legendary solo, *My Gal Sal,* crooned to my mother on bended knee. For the most part, pride outweighed embarrassment even though the concept of amorous parents is a shudder-inducing horror for any child.

By the time Molly and John were born, Mighty Mouse had been replaced by a family station wagon and Dad's gray Rambler was parked where Max once brayed for his supper. The cars no longer danced. Raising four kids under the age of seven required excessive footwork even for my mother.

Our serenading car rides probably began in 1964 as a spill-over from our school bus rides. Like everyone in the nation, we were swept away by the tidal wave of Beatlemania and sang *All My Loving, I Wanna Hold Your Hand,* and *She Loves You* every day between school and home. Even my parents who thought the Fab Four's haircuts were "ghastly" had to admit their harmonies and songwriting were genius.

Singing was a way to speed the 2 1/2 hour trip to Loon Mountain on winter Saturdays and served the added blessing of distracting me from a turbulent tummy after downing butter crunch donuts supplied by Mom in the pre-dawn darkness. Mandy's and my scrawny legs were folded into the back seat where we were surrounded by ski poles, jackets,gloves,and hats. Molly and John were relegated to the "way back"—a pull-up seat facing backwards into the disappearing miles.

We usually began by singing rounds. *Frere Jacques* was our warm-up. I wondered what my five year old brother was picturing as he bellowed the words "Sunny Lematina". We progressed to *White Coral Bells,* a round I still find lilting and sweet. Mom and Dad teamed with Molly and John to bolster the melody but Mandy and I could mostly hold our own without drifting. *Scotland Burning* was the one exception, rendering us hysterical as it accelerated toward the frenzied chorus.

"Fire! Fire! Fire! Fire!" must have been disconcerting sung in Dad's ear on the super highway but he consistently sported an air of bemusement, observing how lucky we were to have siblings. As an only child, he had journeyed too many silent miles alone in the back seat.

We all loved the infamous orchestra song. John was assigned the one note horn, "The horn, the horn. They shout it out."

Dad took over the bass, "The drum has no trouble, just double the double. Five one. One five. Five five five one."

I hogged the soprano violin melody and made sure Mandy or Molly was stuck with that insipid excuse for a rhyme, "The clarinet, the clarinet goes dua, dua, dua, duadet," or the goofy, blaring trumpet which immediately pulverized us into a laughing heap. The result was cacophonous and hilarious. I miss that blend of voices more than I can express.

We also sang favorites from our elementary school songbook. I've searched in vain for that K-6 series containing classics from America and around the world. In my foggy subconscious the cover is a different color for each grade with the word "land" somewhere in the title. If I ever find it again, I will buy up the series. The kindergarten standards were *Go Tell Aunt Rhody* and *Marching to Pretoria*—strange theme songs for five year olds now that I think about it. Our chipper, young voices rang out the sweet strains of a dead gray goose before devolving into "the goslings are mourning because their mother's dead." How did our kindergarten teacher countenance this sort of morbidity warbled by innocents? Almost as odd was our fervent marching to the mysterious Pretoria, an African capitol overtaken during the Boer War.

Other favorites were *Erie Canal, Sweet Betsy from Pike,* and anything by Stephen Foster. Raised in Louisville, Dad could never sing *My Old Kentucky Home* without choking up.

We whipped through songs of exotic birds from strange lands, *Kookaburra* and *Yellow Bird.* We argued over the pronunciation of Fel-da-ri, Fel-da-rah versus Val-da-ri, Val-da-rah, the *Happy Wanderer* having lost something in translation in his hike from the Alps to the 'burbs. We loved to shout the "Ah-hahahahas" out the car windows.

If one of us invited a friend, the discomfort of the cramped quarters was far outweighed by the increased giddiness of our mood. Our guests always seemed to enjoy the singing and, in a few cases, contributed permanent additions to the family repertoire. To this day, if I hum the tender melody of a song called *Four Leaf Clover,* I am transported to the last day of seventh grade, when my mother drove me and a horde of classmates to the beach and a friend taught us this song.

No one believes me when I tell them our annual drive from Boston to Florida was a total blast. Besides the excitement of stopping at restaurants for every meal, there were state lines to be crossed and routes to be debated. The Tappan Zee or the George Washington? The beltway around D.C. or straight through the city? The further south we went, the warmer the weather and the greetings of waitresses and gas station attendants. We welcomed the first Stuckey's restaurant, the signs for Virginia peanuts and North Carolina fireworks, and, of course, the tacky humor of Pedro counting down the miles to the South of the Border motel complex. ("Chile today, hot tamale. You never sausage a place.") Like most travelers of the eastern corridor, we only succumbed once to the lure of Pedro's invitation to dine, quickly discovering his food was as tasteless as his jokes.

As we sang our way to our favorite stop, the Pirate House in Savannah, we mined our show tune collection from *The*

Music Man and *Mary Poppins* to *Camelot, My Fair Lady, The Sound of Music,* and the beautiful Frank Loesser music from *Hans Christian Andersen.*

I always nixed attempts to resurrect Girl Scout favorites like *John Jacob Jingleheimer Schmidt* or *Make New Friends.* They all gave me a headache except for *My Grandfather's Clock* which just plain gave me the creeps. I was freaked out by that chorus, "Ninety years without slumbering. TICK TOCK, TICK TOCK. His life seconds numbering. TICK TOCK, TICK TOCK. It stopped short never to go again when the old man died." I'm still scared of grandfather clocks.

Pulling into mossy, magnolia-lined Savannah at twilight, we would wrap as we always did with *Down in the Old Cherry Orchard,* another of Dad's college solos. His smooth bass resonated from the depths of his southern roots, nudging grins to our faces. His singing would later work the same delight in nine grandchildren around a campfire under the stars in Maine but that was many miles and family memories down the road.

CHAPTER TWELVE

THE TENNIS LADIES

I think I'll miss you most of all.

Dorothy to the Scarecrow in *The Wizard of Oz*
Screenplay by Langley, Ryerson, and Wolf,
adapted from the book by L. Frank Baum

Last week, I wandered back to the woods and hills of my childhood to share the familiar trails and memory-laden vistas with my best friend. Daffodils peered tentatively from the riverbanks, buttoned up tight like us in our jackets, hopeful but unconvinced by the mild air. We New Englanders are wary celebrants, skittish whiplash survivors perpetually catapulted from giddy spring back to cruel winter.

As we dodged mud puddles in the parking lot of the trail head, the sunlight shimmered on the town tennis courts, stopping me in my tracks. A lone Recreation Department worker whistled as he installed new nets for the season. Scenes from my childhood came flooding back.

In my earliest memories, the raising of the tennis nets meant the arrival of spring. This was the day my mother and her best friends, all of whom had been cooped up through endless baby-boom winters in houses bursting with four, five, and six children, took to the courts. When word burned through the Tennis Lady phone lines that the nets were up, all of us pre-schoolers were herded into seatbelt-less station wagons driven by mothers hurtling towards freedom. In the parking lot, our moms chirped and chattered like the returning chickadees as they loosened the screws of wooden tennis presses wound up tight for the winter. We doubles team descendants were corralled to a nearby sandbox. The giddy moms shed us as fast as their coats and raced to play.

Each year, a toddler new to the annual ritual would let out a futile whimper in protest of the sudden maternal exodus. The rest of us knew it was no good. Not whining, not wind, nor the lingering snow in the shadows of the back courts could block the allure of blue sky and the chance to whack the winter out of an unsuspecting tennis ball.

We bonded during those sandbox years until, one by one, we aged out to elementary school, replaced by a stream of younger siblings. When, finally, the youngest after-thought graduated to kindergarten, the tennis schedule became easier for our moms to plan. The weekly game endured and its resulting friendships became the background of our lives. These matches were more than just games. They were companionship, support, and joy in the face of life's challenges. The resilience our mothers found in each other's company was evident on the court. They gathered at the net to discuss gardens, recipes, child crises, college decisions, wedding plans, and, eventually, grandchildren. And, oh, how they laughed! As Dad announced in his fortieth wedding anniversary toast with Mom's best friends beaming in the crowd, "The decades of friendship with these tennis ladies are what life is all about."

In later years, raising my own kids nearby, I was sometimes asked to play as a substitute in the venerable group. By this point, the tennis warm-up was a mere interruption of the gathering at the net to share the week's news and general hilarity. I remember once a group of intense, young hard-bodies on the next court looking scornfully at the frivolity. They couldn't know the noble spirit and persistence required by one of our group just to be out there and how much her soul depended on it.

These were my mother's best friends who sustained not only each other, but me, through the loss of their partner. At Mom's service, they arranged the flower baskets and planned the food. They smiled and encouraged from the pews as they always had from the other side of the net.

The weekly games are no more but the joy they inspire renews me. I share my story with my friend as we turn like daffodils to the sun.